Free For All

Galatians

by

Phillip D. Jensen
&
Kel Richards

St Matthias Press
Sydney • London

Free For All
© St Matthias Press, 1994

St Matthias Press
PO Box 225
KINGSFORD NSW 2032
AUSTRALIA
Ph: (02) 663 1478 Fax: (02) 662 4289

St Matthias Press
PO Box 665
LONDON SW20 8RU
ENGLAND
Ph: (081) 947 5686 Fax: (081) 944 7091

ISBN 1 875245 27 8

Typesetting and design by St Matthias Press.

Contents

How to make the most of these studies...........5

1 Damned angels and gospel twisters 9
2 Under attack 17
3 Faith + anything = nothing.............................25
4 From curse to blessing 31
5 Turning back the clock? 39
6 Christians: slaves or free? 45
7 Unnatural acts 51
8 Two ways to live 59

How to make the most of these studies

1. What is an Interactive Bible Study?

These 'interactive' Bible studies are a bit like a guided tour of a famous city.

The studies will take you through Paul's letter to the Galatians, pointing out things along the way, filling in background details, and suggesting avenues for further exploration. But there is also time for you to do some sight-seeing of your own—to wander off, have a good look for yourself, and form your own conclusions.

In other words, we have designed these studies to fall half-way between a sermon and a set of unadorned Bible study questions.

We want to provide stimulation and input and point you in the right direction, while leaving you to do a lot of the exploration and discovery yourself.

We hope that these studies will stimulate a lot of 'interaction'—interaction with the Bible, with the teaching material, with your own ideas, with other people in discussion, and with God as you talk to him about it all.

2. The format

Each study focuses on a slice of Galatians, and contains teaching material to introduce, summarize, suggest and provoke. We've left plenty of room in the margins for you to jot down questions and comments as you read.

Interspersed throughout the teaching are three types of 'interaction', each with its own symbol:

For starters
Questions to help you think about society and your own experience, in a way that tunes you in to the issues being raised by the Bible passage.

Investigate

Questions to help you investigate key parts of the Bible.

Think it through

Questions to help you think through the implications of your discoveries, and write down your own thoughts and reactions.

When you come to one of these symbols, you'll know that it's time to do some work of your own.

3. Suggestions for individual study

- Before you begin, pray that God will open your eyes to what he is saying in Galatians and give you the strength to do something about it.
- Work through the study, following the directions as you go. Write in the spaces provided.
- Resist the temptation to skip over the *For starters, Investigate* and *Think it through* sections. Writing these things down is a very valuable way to get the mental muscles working.
- Take what opportunities you can to talk to others about what you've learned.

4. Suggestions for group study

- It is *vital* that group members work through the study before the group meets (so everyone will need their own copy of this study guide).
- Spend most of the group time discussing the 'interactive' sections—*For starters, Investigate,* and *Think it through*.
- The role of the group leader is to direct the course of the discussion and to try to draw the threads together at the end.
- We haven't included an 'answer guide' to the questions in the studies. This is a deliberate move—we want to give you a guided tour of Galatians, not a lecture.

(If you would like some additional input, there is a series of tapes available that expound Galatians. For details see inside the back cover.)

5. Getting started

Before you launch into the first study, it's worth taking time to read right through Galatians. It's not very long, and will take you less than half and hour.

Write down a sentence that sums up the main message you got from reading Galatians.

When you have completed these interactive Bible studies, do this exercise again and compare the results to see what sort of journey of discovery God has led you through.

1   Damned angels and gospel twisters

Galatians 1:1-10

For starters

People often think that we can never be certain about the answers to religious questions such as 'Who is God?'. Why is this, do you think?

What answers do people give to the question: 'What is a Christian?'

How would you answer that question?

What is a Christian?

Is the answer just a matter of opinion? Our world today thinks that this question—and many others like it—is just a matter of opinion.

The world today is more lost than ever on the subject of what can and can't be known. There is a great lack of confidence about what is certain, as more and more things fall into the category of 'relative'.

Today no one is right—except the person who says 'no one is right': he is always right!

Every point of view is tolerated today, except the view that says there is right and wrong, true and false.

But in Galatians we will discover that God says that following Jesus Christ is not just a matter of opinion. There is a right, there is a wrong—there is true, there is false—about Christianity.

Investigate

Read Galatians 1:8-9

1. What tone does Paul adopt when discussing the preachers of a "different gospel"?

2. Why can't there be more than one gospel? Why is it such a serious issue?

3. What clues do you find here to the problems in the Galatian church?

1. The problem of confusion

Galatia is Turkey, roughly speaking. The exact geographical boundaries wobble around a bit, but what Paul called Galatia is, more or less, part of modern Turkey.

Paul had preached the gospel in Galatia, and founded churches there. He is writing to these churches because something has happened—troublers have come among them: "Evidently some people are throwing you into confusion and are trying to pervert the gospel of Christ" (v.7).

Who were these troublers? They were people who were confusing what it means to be a Christian.

As we shall see later in Galatians, they were attacking Paul and the gospel by insisting on obedience to the Jewish law, as symbolised in circumcision.

For the Jew in the Old Testament (from Genesis 17 onwards), circumcision (the surgical removal of the foreskin of the penis) was the sign of being 'under contract' with God, the contract that gave rise to the law. Circumcision was the symbol of accepting the Old Testament law as the system that ruled your life. This is stated in Galatians 5:3: "Again I declare to every man who lets himself be circumcised that he is required to obey the whole law".

But these Turks were Gentiles (non-Jews) and they were uncircumcised—they had never taken the law upon themselves. Can these non-Jews become Christians without becoming Jews first? That is the question the 'troublers' were using to confuse the Galatians.

At first glance, this question has nothing much to do with us. But in these studies we shall find the same type of mistake being made today that the 'troublers' made back in the first century.

2. Paul's unusual greeting

Every culture has standard forms of greetings to use in letters. For example, today we might write:

Dear Aunt Agatha,
    Thank you for the Christmas present—an elephant's foot umbrella stand is just what I have always wanted.
                                                    Yours sincerely,
                                                    Frank

The first century had a standard form for letters that went like this:

i.   The writer's name
ii.   The people to whom he was writing
iii.   Greetings!

You can see this standard form throughout the New Testament. However, the Christian form was slightly different—instead of 'Greetings!', Christians would write 'Grace and peace to you!'.

Paul also had his own standard letter form. It generally went like this:

i.   Paul, an apostle of Jesus Christ
ii.   To the church in ...
iii.   Grace and peace to you
iv.   I always thank God for you because of ...
v.   And I am praying for you ...

Investigate

Read Galatians 1:1-10

1. In what ways does Paul's greeting differ from his standard greeting (above)?

2. What does Paul say about what it means for him to be an apostle (v.1)?

3. What does Paul say about the source of "grace and peace"?

4. Paul is astonished that the Galatians are deserting the gospel of Christ (v.6). What do we learn about the gospel of Christ in this passage (vv.1-10)?

3. What is the gospel?

The giving

The key word here is grace (verses 3 and 6), and it means 'generosity'. It is the opposite to something we have earned, something we do for ourselves.

If, at the end of a week's work your boss gives you a week's pay, that is not generosity; it is just what you have earned—what you deserve or merit because of what you have done. But if you don't turn up for work and the boss still hands you a packet of money—that is grace. That is surprising (astonishing!) generosity, and is entirely unearned.

Grace and merit are opposites. You cannot get something both by grace and by merit at the same time. It is either one or the other. You either earn something or you are given it—it can't be both at the same time.

And grace—astonishing generosity—is what we get from Jesus. Paul wants to drive home that Jesus "gave himself for our sins to rescue us from the present evil age" (v.4).

The Galatians are turning away from God who has called them through this astonishing generosity—this self giving—of Jesus Christ (vv. 6-7).

The deserting

"I am astonished", writes Paul in verse 6, "that you are so quickly deserting the one who called you by the grace of Christ and are turning to a different gospel."

Verses 7, 8 and 9 then tell us some amazing things about the character of the gospel that makes the idea that 'all religious truth is just a matter of opinion' absolute nonsense.

In these verses, the point is that there is only one true gospel—the gospel of the grace of Jesus Christ. But, there are also 'gospel twisters'—people who try to pervert (or twist) the gospel of grace.

And Paul makes another point: the authority of the gospel rests in the gospel message itself—not in the preacher of the gospel, however impressive that preacher might be. Don't even trust an angelic preacher, says Paul, only trust the one true gospel of grace.

So, if an angel (or an apostle!) tries to sell you a different gospel, says Paul, tell them to go to hell!

Investigate

1. What reasons does Paul give for being so insistent on the gospel of grace?

2. Which words (that Paul uses) convey the importance that Paul attaches to the gospel of grace?

3. When this letter was read for the first time, what did verses 1-10 tell the Galatian Christians about themselves?

4. Drawing the line

There is only one gospel—the gospel of the grace, the self-giving, of Jesus. There is no other gospel. It is either this or nothing.

"That's intolerant!", comes the protest.

Yes! God is intolerant about untruth.

Is it tolerant to say that the earth is both flat and round? There are some issues where 'tolerance' amounts to foolishness, and the truth of the gospel is one of them.

If Jesus Christ is God—then Krishna isn't. And Allah isn't. That's exactly the same as saying that if the world is round, then it isn't flat.

In Galatians, God is telling us that there is no other gospel. There is no other way back home. It is this or nothing.

Think it through

1. How would you answer the person who says, "Religion is just a matter of opinion. People should believe whatever is true for them."

2. How does Paul's 'drawing the line' (in verses 8 and 9) affect the way we share the gospel with our friends from other religious backgrounds?

3. What guidelines does Galatians 1:1-10 give us for exposing counterfeits of Christianity?

4. From Galatians 1:1-10 write down the characteristics of the true gospel.

5. Discuss any experiences you have had where people have tried to pervert this gospel.

6. How faithful have you been to the one true gospel? (In your conversations with non-Christians have you been tempted make it more palatable? Have you been tempted to trim the gospel to make it more attractive to your listeners?)

2 Under attack

Galatians 1:11-2:10

For starters

1. What kinds of attacks on Christianity do you hear today?

2. Have you ever been attacked for being a Christian? If so, how did you handle it?

3. Was it you or was it the gospel under attack?

4. How did this show itself?

1. Paul under attack

Attacks on the gospel message—and its messengers—often have the benefit of clarifying the issues involved in the gospel. For example, Paul was attacked for not being a proper Apostle, and for not being a proper Jew. These attacks drove Paul to explain the source of his gospel message and of his commission to spread that message. They also pushed Paul to explain the relationship between being Christian and being Jewish.

Investigate

Read Galatians 1:11-2:10

1. Where did Paul get his gospel from? (1:12)

2. Before his conversion, which Christian preachers explained the gospel to Paul?

3. What evidence does Paul give to prove his Jewishness?

4. What was unusual about Paul's conversion? (Compare 1:16 with Acts 26:12-18)

5. Why did Paul go to Jerusalem the first time? (1:18)

6. Why did he go to Jerusalem the second time? (2:2)

7. Whom does Paul report meeting with in Jerusalem?

on the first visit (1:18-19)

on another visit (2:1-2, 6-9)

2. Paul's response

Paul did not insist that Gentiles be circumcised, nor did he insist that they follow the Jewish rules about eating—rules that spelled out who you could eat with, when, where and how.

All this upset 'the troublers' who (apparently) claimed that what Paul did was different to what the 'big name' apostles in Jerusalem did.

Paul's response was twofold.

1. He said that he was not under the authority of the 'big name' apostles in Jerusalem. The gospel, said Paul, had come to him directly by revelation from God, and, hence, he was under God's authority, not the authority of other apostles.

2. He said that what he preached was in full fellowship with the Jerusalem authorities. Although Paul was independent of the Jerusalem authorities, his message was the same as theirs: it was the true gospel.

Paul makes the point that before his conversion he did not hear the gospel from any Christian preacher. Indeed, before his conversion Paul's only contact with Christians was to persecute them (1:13,14)! In fact, Paul did not hear the gospel from any human being (1:12). Then, says Paul, God himself revealed the gospel to me (1:15), and he did so in order that "I might preach him (Jesus) among the Gentiles" (1:16).

Immediately after his conversion Paul went off to preach the gospel in Arabia—without bothering to check whether he had any human permission to do so (1:17)!

Paul did (eventually) go to Jerusalem to talk to the big wigs— the first time 3 years after his conversion (1:18), and again 14 years later (2:1).

He went because God told him to go. Paul's concern was that

he might run his race in vain (2:2). This may mean that he was worried that those who thought Christians needed to be Jewish would ruin his work. It seems likely that, by coming to Jerusalem to present his gospel message, Paul was actually checking out the authenticity of the Jerusalem Christians, rather than the other way around!

Investigate

Read Galatians 2:6-10

1. What did Paul set out to explain at his meeting with James, Peter and John? (2:2)

2. What conclusion did James, Peter and John come to about the place in God's work given to Paul?

3. What did they base this on?

4. In looking at the mission field, how did the apostles see God at work in Paul and in Peter (and the others)?

Think it through

1. If you were criticized for not believing in the authentic gospel of God's free grace, how would you defend yourself?

2. How can we make sure that the true gospel is being preached in our churches?

3. God's gospel

During Paul's visit to Jerusalem he had with him an uncircumcised Christian—Titus. Paul resisted attempts to compel Titus to be circumcised. Why? "So that the truth of the gospel might remain with you" (2:5).

This was Paul drawing the line.

The circumcision of Titus, he said, was a matter of the gospel itself—it was fundamental, not a 'side issue'.

So, was Titus circumcised? The truth is that we don't know! All we know is that he wasn't compelled to be circumcised. He might, like Timothy (Acts 16:3) have chosen to be circumcised if that would assist his gospel ministry. But it is more than likely that he was not.

The point is that there is a world of difference between being compelled to be circumcised (or baptised, or taking part in any religious ceremony) as a legalistic requirement to be saved—and choosing freely to be circumcised (or baptised, or whatever) to facilitate ministry.

The issue of circumcision highlights the greatness of the gospel. Law keeping is not the way to God. The way to God is through God's way to us—namely Jesus, who died for our forgiveness. The way to God is not by being 'good', but being forgiven!

That is God's gospel, which is the only gospel there is.

Paul knew that it was worth being attacked over this issue. He stood firmly for the gospel, in order that the truth would remain in the worldwide church. We need to follow Paul's example. If drawing the line means being attacked for what we believe, even by those who (falsely) claim to be our brothers and sisters (2:4), so be it. We must never jeopardise the truth of the gospel of free grace.

Think it through

1. Is there any part of church life that should be considered essential to salvation?

2. Do any of your church's rituals or customs jeopardise the gospel of God's free grace?

3. The Rev Matt Johnson is minister at St Basil's-by-the-Abattoir, where he preaches the sermon every Sunday morning. Matt has decided to stop wearing clerical robes because he feels that robes make him seem 'holier' than the congregation. Some members say they like his casual approach, others complain that by wearing ordinary clothes he is not respecting his position.
Should Matt wear clerical robes? Give your reasons.

3. Is the true gospel of God's free grace at stake in his decision? Give your reasons.

4. What circumstances might make this a genuine gospel issue?

3 Faith + anything = nothing

Galatians 2:11-21

For starters

Surveys show that the vast majority of people still believe in God. In your view, how do most people think they can get right with God and be accepted by him?

1. The war with the law

The big challenge to the gospel in Paul's day and in our day is the same—it is law-keeping—and Galatians is about the struggle between the true gospel of the free grace of God and law keeping.

Study 1 showed us the gospel of grace, and Paul's concern that the Galatian Christians were deserting it. Study 2 examined Paul's claim to preach the true gospel, and how he was attacked over his refusal to bow to pressure to circumcise Titus.

In this next section of Galatians, we will see Paul further explaining the enormous difference between law-keeping and the gospel. The difference is apparent in a number of ways, but this letter deals with it chiefly in relation to circumcision (2:3) and food rules (2:12).

Prior to the writing of Galatians, the two apostles—Peter and Paul—had clashed in Antioch (Gal 2:11), where the first Gentile church had met. The cause of the conflict was the relationship between Jewish and Gentile Christians and, in particular, Peter's decision to stop eating with the Gentile Christians. To understand something of Peter's background to this clash, we need to turn to Acts 10.

Investigate

Read Acts 10

1. Why did Peter have doubts about eating certain foods?

2. Before the vision, why would Peter have been reluctant to visit Cornelius' house? (v.28)

3. What was so surprising to the Jewish (the 'circumcised') Christians? (v.45)

4. Why did Peter baptise Cornelius and his family? (v.47, and Acts 11:17)

By the time of Paul's letter to the Galatians, there were Christian Jews and non-Jews, who had once been poles apart, calling each other 'brother' and 'sister'.

But what sort of members of the Christian church could non-Jews be? Full members? Or only associate members? And if they were to be full members, did this mean they had to take on the whole of Judaism as well? Like not eating certain foods? Like being circumcised?

In the last study we looked at the significance of circumcision for the truth of the gospel. In Galatians 2:11-21, the focus is on eating. But once again, in this historical circumstance, the issue that is really being wrestled with is law-keeping versus the good news of God's free gift in Jesus Christ.

Investigate

Read Galatians 2:11-21

1. Why did Peter stop eating with the non-Jewish Christians in Antioch?

2. Why did Paul confront Peter over this issue?

3. Paul is writing to the Galatians, telling them of his confrontation with Peter in Antioch, because it has direct bearing on their own struggles with law-keeping. Just as Peter's actions weren't "in line with the truth of the gospel", so Paul is beginning to build his argument that those who are troubling the Galatians are also not acting in line with the gospel. In vv. 15-21, he proceeds to spell out what it is about the gospel that made Peter's treatment of his Gentile brothers so inappropriate. What do these verses say about:

• how we are *not* justified before God (that is, declared right with him)

- how we *can* be justified

- the relationship of the Christian to the law

- the consequences of going back to law-keeping

4. How does all this show Peter's actions to be wrong?

5. Fill in the following table from vv. 15-21:

	At the start of the Christian life	Throughout the Christian life
The place of the law		
The place of faith in Christ		

Today's challenge

The temptation to withdraw from table fellowship with Gentile Christians because of Jewish food laws, is not one that most Christians today have to deal with. To start with, most of us are Gentiles.

However, the temptation is always with us to see some form of law-keeping as the way to get right with God, or to *stay* right with God.

In terms of getting right with God, it is frighteningly common to hear people speak of the Ten Commandments or the Sermon on the Mount or some other ethical standard as being the way to get right with God. If we make a reasonable fist of keeping these and being good, they say, then God is bound to accept us in the end.

However, this sort of thinking betrays a low view of God and the law, and a high view of ourselves. We need to realise that the God we are seeking to please is a consuming fire, an awe-inspiring God of blindingly pure holiness who cannot tolerate any sin. He is no easy God to please. What is worse, despite our best intentions, we are all woeful at law-keeping. When we actually compare our behaviour with the Ten Commandments or the Sermon on the Mount, we come up embarrasingly short.

For Christians—that is, for those of us who have realised how far short we fall and have cast ourselves on Jesus Christ—there is still a danger in law-keeping. Having abandoned the law as a means of being right before God, there is no going back. It is not as if, having been declared right with God through Jesus' death alone, we then take up a regime of observing the law in order to remain Christians. In Paul's words, we cannot rebuild what we have destroyed. By trusting in Christ for our righteousness, we have utterly abandoned the path of law-keeping. We have died to it, says Paul. That part of us has been crucified with Christ, and our new life with Christ is lived out in trusting him (i.e. faith).

This was Peter's mistake. By drawing back from full fellowship with his Gentile brothers, he was going back to the law. He was trying to resurrect what was dead and buried; he was trying to rebuild what he had destroyed when he trusted in Christ. To attempt to add law-keeping to faith was to destroy what faith was all all about.

Think it through

1. In what ways can we as Christians be tempted to get right with God through rules and law-keeping or good works?

2. Is the motivation different for keeping God's laws for Christians and non-Christians?

3. How does Christ's death demonstrate the inadequacy of law-keeping as a way to heaven?

4. Many, perhaps most, non-Christians think that law-keeping (or some vague attempt at it) is the way to get right with God. Write down a short, point-by-point plan for explaining the gospel of God's free grace to a friend who thinks this way.

4

From curse to blessing

Galatians 3:1-18

For starters

How do most people think about Jesus (when they stop to give him any serious thought at all)? What are they likely to say about Jesus?

1. The cursed Jesus

Jesus was a common criminal, a blasphemer, a phoney and a failure.

At least, that is what Paul thought when his name was still Saul and he was busy persecuting Christians.   Saul/Paul believed that Jesus had obviously been cursed by God.   The evidence was that he had been executed—crucified. Saul/Paul knew that the Bible said that "Cursed is everyone who is hung on a tree" (v.13, quoting Deut 21:23).

To Saul/Paul, Jesus was a disaster area! To call him the Christ, the Messiah, was perverse and peculiar. This assessment underwent a radical transformation when he went to Damascus to persecute Christians living there. Because on the road he met the 'cursed' Jesus, risen from the dead. And his whole way of thinking about life was radically transformed by that revelation.

The persecutor became the proclaimer, and went about preaching the gospel that he had tried to exterminate. It was this redeemed and reformed Paul who stood up in front of the Galatians and by his words clearly portrayed Jesus Christ as crucified (v.1b).

2. A three-stage argument

Under the preaching of the transformed Paul many people were themselves transformed, including the people in Galatia to whom Paul is writing this letter.

But after Paul moved on, and the "law keepers" we learned about in Study 3 came on the scene, the Galatians lost the plot. Paul reminds them here that it was by believing the gospel of God's free grace through Jesus Christ—not observing the law— that they received the Holy Spirit. He supports this statement with a three-pronged argument and an example.

Investigate

Read Galatians 3:1-14

Stage 1: The argument from experience. (vv.1-5)

Paul first reminds the Galatians of their past reality, of what happened when they first received the gospel.

1. What answer is Paul expecting to the question he asks in verse 2?

2. According to verse 2, at what point in a Christian's life is he/she filled with the Holy Spirit? Is it:
   • When he/she believes the gospel of the crucified and risen Jesus?
   • When he/she is perfectly obedient to God?
   • When other Christians "lay hands" on him/her?
   • Some other point in the Christian life?
   • Impossible to say?

3. What are the Galatians now trying to add to belief in the gospel message they heard?

4. What does that make them in Paul's eyes?

5. Why have these Galatians needed to call on the courage and endurance that the Spirit gives?

6. What evidence of the work of the Spirit have these Galatians seen with their own eyes?

Stage 2: The argument from Abraham. *(vv.6-9)*

As he does in Romans, Paul then turns to Abraham, the Father of the Jews, as an ally in his argument against 'law' as a way to be righteous.

1. Abraham's righteousness: on what basis did Abraham receive the miraculous gift of righteousness? (v.6, and check out the passage Paul is quoting here, Gen 15:6)

2. Abraham's children: What defining characteristic identifies a person as a true descendant of Abraham?

3. Abraham's blessing: The Scriptures knew that blessing would flow through Abraham, but who receives this blessing? (vv.8-9, and check out the passages being referred to here, Gen 12:3, 18:18 and 22:18)

4. How does Abraham's blessing—the miraculous gift of righteousness—come?

Stage 3: The argument from Christ. (vv.10-14)

1. What is the immediate contrast between verses 10 and 11?

Through _____ we receive _____

Through _____ we receive _____

2. Why is this?

3. How much of the law do you have to keep to avoid the curse of the law?

4. Why is no-one justified by law?

5. How are faith and law opposed?

6. How does Jesus redeem us?

7. Why did Jesus redeem us?

8. How does verse 14 summarize the whole argument (from 1-13)?

Jesus buys us out of the curse of the law—by becoming cursed
himself, in our place. He redeems us—pays a ransom for us.
How? By being "hung on a tree", says Paul—arguing from
Scripture. Paul has come full circle, back to the same idea that
obsessed him when he was Saul, persecutor of Christians. But
now he understands that Jesus suffered that curse on our behalf!

3. Being in the Spirit

It is worth pausing to consider what this passage teaches us
about receiving the Spirit.

First, notice the centrality of the cross of Jesus.

You can't get around the cross. The only way to receive the
Spirit is by faith in the cross of Christ. It is through Jesus suffering
our curse and being executed that we are redeemed and filled
with the Holy Spirit. This is how we start with the Spirit and this
is how we finish—it is all through Christ crucified.

Second, notice that receiving the Spirit is part of God's historic plan.

There are not two gospels, nor two plans of God. God didn't
start down one track in the Old Testament and then revert to plan
B in the New Testament. His plan to pour out his Spirit on his
people went all the way back to his promises to Abraham. Notice
how the passage describes God's promise to Abraham as "the
gospel announced in advance" (v. 8).

Third, notice that the Spirit is for all the nations.

In fulfilment of the promise to Abraham, God has included all
people—Jews and Gentiles—in his plan. The Spirit comes to all
who abandon human effort and put their trust in Jesus Christ
crucified.

4. An example: giving by promise

To make his point clear Paul now illustrates his three-fold argument with an example from how a human contract such as inheritance works (we'll look further at the notion of inheritance in the next study).

Investigate

Read Galatians 3:15-18

1. What was the basis of God's dealings with Abraham?

2. To whom were the promises spoken? (v.16)

To _____ (a)
And to _____ (b)

3. Who is (b)? (v.16)

4. Can God's covenant contract—his promise—be nullified by the law?

5. What does our inheritance depend on?

Think it through

1. What would cause Paul to write to you: "Oh foolish Christian!"? What is likely to cause you to lose the plot and take your eyes off the gospel?

2. What kinds of rules and regulations are today's Christians tempted to elevate to a way to God?

3. List some rules that people have told you that you should follow in order to be a 'real' Christian, or a 'serious' Christian.

5 Turning back the clock?

Galatians 3:18-4:11

For starters

When you become an adult, how does your attitude to the rules you had to keep as a child change?

1. The purpose of the law

So far in Galatians, we have been onlookers to a battle between 'law' and 'faith'. Paul has been vigorously defending the gospel of grace from attack by those who would require Gentile Christians to fully obey the OT law.

No-one is justified by law-keeping, Paul has thundered. There is only one way to be declared right with God, and that is through Christ's death on the cross. It is the only way, and if you try to add law-keeping to faith, as an additional requirement, you have misunderstood the whole thing and destroyed the very essence of faith. The blessings promised to Abraham flow out to the Gentiles through faith, not through the law. If you want to be a true Jew, a true child of Abraham, then receive the promise by faith, just as Abraham did. This has been Paul's argument up to this point.

All this leaves one big question hanging: What purpose *does* the Old Testament law serve? If the Spirit was not poured out through law-keeping, but through the gospel of grace, then why did God bring in the law in the first place? What place does the law have for the Christian life?

It is to this question that Paul now turns in his letter.

Investigate

Read Galatians 3:18-4:7

1. What does Paul say is the purpose of the law? (v. 19, 24)

2. The law was "added" until…when? Note down the different ways this 'when' is described.

3. Who is the 'Seed'? (v. 19)

4. In vv. 25-29, Paul switches from talking about 'we' and 'us' to talking about 'you'.

   Who do you think are the 'we'?

   Who are the 'you'?

5. Now that the law is no longer operational (as a guardian or gaol-keeper), what does this do to the barriers between Jews and Gentiles?

6. Who can now be one of Abraham's offspring ('seed') and how?

2. Sons not slaves

In the section we've been reading, Paul uses several images to describe the place and purpose of the Old Testament law. He calls it a gaol-keeper who kept God's people locked up or restrained until Christ came. He calls it a school-teacher or child-minder (this is what the Greek word in verse 24 means; the NIV renders it "put in charge"). He calls it a guardian and trustee.

These are images that Paul's readers would have well understood. In the ancient world, it was common for a well-educated slave to be put in charge of the 'son and heir' of a wealthy family. This slave would train, teach, discipline and exercise complete control over the child. Then, when childhood and youth were past, and the young man was of age, he would come into his inheritance. Then their positions would be reversed. The slave would now be under the command of the heir.

All these images emphasize that the law God gave to Old Testament Israel was a temporary measure. Its role was to restrain and educate; to put a brake on sinfulness and set boundaries inside which God's people could live until Christ came. Its function was never to save or justify, says Paul. Now that faith in Christ has come, the law is no longer in charge. It is no longer a supervisor. We are no longer slaves, but sons and heirs.

In all of this, we must remember that the people who were troubling the Galatian church were from a Jewish background. They were trying to persuade the Galatians that, whether they were Jewish or not, they needed to keep the whole Old Testament law if they were going to be genuine Christians.

In reply to these troublers, Paul is saying that the Old Testament law was a temporary measure in God's plan. It applied to the Old Testament people of God (the Israelites) until Christ came, but now its supervisory role is over. It is no longer the supervisor—not of Jews any more, and certainly not of Gentiles—because now Christ has come. Now all can inherit the promise to Abraham; now all can be sons of God through trusting in Jesus Christ.

Now, let us read on.

Investigate

Read Galatians 4:1-11*

1. In what sense were the Jews (the "we" of v. 3) under slavery to "basic principles"?

2. What was the time limit to their slavery?

3. How did God free them from their slavery?

4. On what basis can people become 'sons of God'? Is this the same for everyone?

5. What are the privileges of being one of God's sons?

6. In what sense were Paul's Gentile readers (the "you" in v. 8) also at one time under slavery to "principles"?

*Note: These are tricky verses. They are easier to understand if you realise that Paul is using a play on words that doesn't come out so well in the English. The Greek word *stoicheia* that is translated in 4:3 and 4:9 as 'basic principles' can have a variety of meanings. The idea behind the word is of a first or basic thing from which other things follow. It is used to describe the spoken letters of the alphabet, or the natural elements of which the world is made, or the fundamental principles of an art or science. In Colossians 2, Paul uses *stoicheia* to describe the 'natural' principles on which pagan philosophy and religion are built.

In Galatians 4, Paul seems to be using this word in a double sense to make his point.

7. What would going back to law-keeping and religious observances mean for these Gentiles?

3. No turning back

Can you imagine Nelson Mandela, freed from imprisonment after 25 years and now President of South Africa, going back to gaol and asking to be locked up again? Can you imagine a student, finally graduating from university after years of education, re-enrolling in primary school? Can you imagine a street-kid picked up from the gutter and adopted into a warm, accepting family choosing to go back to homelessness?

This is the level of astonishment Paul shows towards the Galatians. He can't believe that they are doing what they are doing. Why go back to slavery? God freed you from all the pagan mumbo-jumbo and religious observances of your old life, and adopted you into his very own family through faith in his Son. Why on earth would you want to go back to law-keeping?

Again and again in this letter to the Galatians, we have been taught these sorts of things. The gospel of God's grace in Christ has freed us from the slavery of law. It has freed us from being 'religious' and trying to please God through doing certain things— whether they are the things of God's own Old Testament law, or the things of human religion.

The Old Testament law was certainly part of God's plan. It served an important function. But now that Christ has come, its supervisory role has ended. It no longer is in power over God's people. We are no longer children in slavery. Now we are heirs.

Think it through

1. Why are the trappings of religion so attractive to people? What is it about law-keeping that appeals?

2. In what ways are Christians today tempted to 'go back to slavery' regarding:

- keeping the Old Testament law?

- keeping other religious rules and laws?

3. If Christians are no longer 'under the law', what role does the Old Testament have for Christians? Look up:

Rom 1:1-2

Rom 4:23-24

Rom 15:4

1 Cor 9:9-10

1 Cor 10:1-13

2 Cor 6:16-7:1

Gal 3:6-9

2 Tim 3:16-17

4. 'The proclamation of the gospel is the death-knell for all religion.' Do you agree with this statement? Why/why not?

6 Christians: slaves or free?

Galatians 4:12-5:12

For starters

List some of the restrictions on freedom that are most often resented in today's societies.

1. Paul and the Galatians

Much of the letter to the Galatians hinges on the relationship between Paul, the Galatians and the 'troublers'. Chapter 4 of Galatians starts to spell this out with some personal anecdotes.

We read that on his initial visit, the Galatians warmly received Paul (4:14). We don't know the details of the illness from which Paul suffered (4:13), or why it led him to preach the gospel there. But, presumably (4:14a) it was something unpleasant for them to deal with—we can only speculate.

The Galatians built up a good friendship with the apostle, treating him with great respect (4:14b). But now, Paul is worried, the Galatians have been stirred up to be 'anti-Paul' (4:16-17).

Investigate

Revision of chapters 1 - 3

1. After Paul's departure, what kind of 'trouble' came to the Galatians?

2. How did the Galatian Christians respond to these 'troublers'?

3. Why has Paul written this letter?

Read Galatians 4:12-20

4. In this passage how does Paul describe his relationship with the Galatians? (4:19-20)

2. Paul's plea

Paul takes such a strong stance here because the issue at stake is the truth. He is concerned for the truth of the gospel of God's free grace. These 'troublers' are not just disturbing a cosy club—they are theologically false and therefore intolerable.

Paul had seen a group of 'slaves' freed, and now these troublers were persuading them back into slavery.

In adopting a life of law-keeping, the Galatians were giving up the freedom that they had found in the gospel of grace. They were giving up their relationship with God—which is true freedom. Paul can't believe it's happening.

Investigate

Read Galatians 4:21-5:12

1. What concerns Paul in 5:1-2?

2. How does the story of Hagar and Sarah help to explain the difference between the Old Covenant and the New Covenant?

3. Why might this have been an especially useful way for Paul to argue his case to the Galatians (4:21)?

3. Abraham's sons

God promised Abraham that, despite their old age, he would heal Sarah's infertility and give Abraham and Sarah a son of their own. Impatient for a child, Sarah gave her husband a slave girl, Hagar, to breed from. And Hagar gave birth to Ishmael. However, God still fulfilled his promise and, in due time, Isaac was born to Sarah.

This story is used by Paul figuratively to represent slavery under law-keeping versus freedom under the gospel.

Ishmael—although temporarily a son and heir—was always a slave, and the son of a slave. His story stands for Mount Sinai, says Paul (4:24)—that is to say, for the law. Slavery is the symbol of the law. Notice the present position of Israel as far as Paul is concerned. The Jews of today (and that includes the State of Israel) are in slavery. They are just like Ishmael, because, as we saw in Study 5, although they are physically the sons of Abraham, they are not true sons of Abraham. They are not the heirs.

Isaac—born of a free woman—is the fulfilment of a promise from God. His story stands for the new covenant—the gospel of the free grace of God in Jesus Christ. Our Jerusalem does not stand on a rocky slope in the state of Israel: our home is the heavenly Jerusalem. And we, like Isaac, are the children of promise—children of supernatural birth:

> Yet to all who received him [Jesus], to those who believed in his name, he gave the right to become children of God—children born not of natural descent, nor of human decision or a husband's will, but born of God.
>
> John 1:12-13

Think it through

1. According to the argument of 4:21-31, who is persecuting whom?

2. In what ways are the 'children of the promise' still persecuted today?

3. In 5:2-6 Paul is saying (in effect) that choosing circumcision means asking God to judge you by his perfect law. Where would that put us in relation to Christ?

4. If faith is all that counts, does that make the Christian life a matter of passively waiting?

5. What possible "yokes of slavery" can you see that might endanger your spiritual freedom?

6. What specific steps can you take to avoid this danger?

7. Could you be in danger of imposing a "yoke of slavery" on other Christians? (5:10b)

8. What specific steps can you take to avoid this danger?

7 Unnatural acts

Galatians 5:13-26

For starters

What kind of behaviour are most people likely to excuse by saying: "Ah well, it's only natural"?

1. Called to be free

In Galatians, God has taught us so far that we have been freed from the burden of law keeping.

That is what we have been freed *from*—but what have we been freed *for*?

Paul started to spell out the answer in verse 6: our faith can "express itself through love". In verse 13 Paul calls this "serving one another in love". This, we are taught, is a summary of the entire law (v.14).

So, is this where the whole argument in Galatians has led us—back to the law?

Investigate

Read Matthew 7:12; 22:34-40; Romans 13:9-10

Explain how the whole law can be summarized by the command to "Love your neighbour as yourself".

2. Law versus love

We are not freed from the law in order to 'freely sin': we are freed from the law in order to love.

But when you love, you wind up obeying the law! The law and love are, in their content, much the same (v.14). If I am serving you in love then I won't tell you a lie, or steal from you, or gossip about you.

Well, if that's the case, then what's the difference between the two? There is a double difference: a difference of motive, and a difference of relationship.

Motive

Motivation, or intention, is part of every action. Picture this scene:

A pretty girl drops an armful of books in front of a library. Three young men rush to pick them up for her: the first because he is a genuine humanitarian who just wants to help; the second because he has been looking at this girl with longing for months and this is his excuse to get an introduction; and the third because he is failing his course and she is top of the class—and this is his chance to plead for a little free coaching.

What they *do* is identical, but they have three different intentions (or motivations).

Relationship

Relationship—our standing or status with others—can also give meaning to our actions. Picture this scene:

Two athletes sprint as hard as they can around the cinder track of the sports oval. One is running hard because he has been selected for the competition team—and he is motivated by his selection to perform at his best. The other is hoping to win team selection. The first is running with a full heart, eager to please the selectors who have chosen him. The second is trying to force the selectors to make a late, additional selection (namely himself), even though it is against the rules.

The difference in relationship colours their actions.

Think it through

Complete the following table, describing (a) the relationship, or standing, before God, and (b) the motivation, or intention, of the Law Keeper versus the Christian (the man or woman of the Spirit).

	Law Keeper	Christian
Relationship with God		
Motive for action		

3. Act naturally?

The New International Version (NIV) of the Bible, which we follow in these Interactive Bible Studies, uses the expression "the sinful nature" (you'll find it in vv.13, 16, 17, 19 and 24). However, other versions (and the NIV footnotes) use the word "flesh".

The Bible's concept of "flesh" differs from the way we would commonly use the word today. For the Bible, "flesh" has to do with living in this fallen, sinful world: "flesh" stands for what we are by nature (which is why the NIV's "sinful nature" is a good translation).

We can see this meaning illustrated in the lists in verses 19-23 where the sinful nature (the flesh) is contrasted with living by the Spirit.

Investigate

Read Galatians 5:19-23

1. Can you think of a short phrase that summarises the list of acts of the sinful nature?

2. Can you think of a short phrase that summarises the fruit of the Spirit?

4. The constant conflict

"So I say", writes Paul, "live by the Spirit, and you will not gratify the desires of the sinful nature (the flesh)" (v.16). Then Paul goes on to describe living naturally (vv.19-21).

There is a constant conflict between our old nature (the desires and urges that are part of our corrupt human nature), and the Spirit now living in us (v.17). The conflict continues for as long as we are in our fleshly bodies.

The only way to get out of the conflict is to get out of our sinful nature. And the only way for that to happen is for Jesus to return, or for us to die. As long as we are here, we will be fighting this battle.

The fight is not 'out there'—it is within each one of us. Have you not felt the urge to be selfishly ambitious? To compete? To be envious? To be jealous? That is living naturally.

Have you never become caught up in a little circle of gossip? A little clique? A little group that includes this one and excludes that one? That is living naturally.

Have you never lost your temper? Had a fit of rage? Spread discord? Created dissension? Hated someone? That is living naturally.

Picture this scene, a true scene this time: a large supermarket had a blackout a few years ago. It lasted only three minutes. In that time hundreds of goods were stolen from all over the shop.

Given the opportunity, ordinary 'honest' people steal. That is living naturally.

Think it through

1. Do "sins of the flesh" only turn up in adult movies? What sins of the flesh might you find in a family movie?

2. If Paul had lost his temper, would he have thought that an unnatural thing to do?

3. Why are ambition, factions and jealousy "works of the flesh"? What impact might they have on the lives of others?

4. Should Christians expect to be able to conquer the sin in their lives?

5. Living unnaturally

We must not live according to our nature, but according to the Spirit (v.16). That is unnatural for us.

The beauty of this is that it is positive.

The law tends to be negative: don't do this, don't do that. Life in the Spirit, on the other hand, is positive: be loving, joyful, peaceful, patient, kind, good, faithful, gentle and self-controlled. We have not been freed in order to indulge our sinful natures, but to serve one another in love. There will be conflict, and we must turn our backs on the works of the flesh.

But positively, there is the fruit of the Spirit. The word "fruit" is singular—it means "a crop", not different "fruits". There are not meant to be "kindness" Christians and "goodness" Christians and "faithfulness" Christians. Rather, the Christian is meant to be producing a crop of all these things.

We are not passive in this process. We are to "keep in step with the Spirit" (v. 25). As we fight the inner conflict, as we turn our backs on the flesh, as we pray and work at the crop of the Spirit, God works in us to produce love, joy, peace, patience, kindness, goodness, gentleness, faithfulness and self-control.

Investigate

1. What happens when people live by the sinful nature and not by the Spirit? (v.15 and v.21)

2. What makes it so easy to recognise the "works of the flesh"—of living naturally?

Think it through

1. Looking at the list of the fruit of the Spirit, which two of those qualities are you best at? Which two do you need to work hardest at?

2. What steps can you take this week to co-operate more with God in growing the crop of the Spirit in your life?

8 Two ways to live

Galatians 6:1-18

For starters

How do you think most people would react to the hard line that Galatians draws between grace and law—between the genuine and the false way to be right with God?

1. Restoration, repayment and reaping

In Galatians, God is teaching us to draw the line: you either trust Jesus or you trust yourself. There are only two ways to live.

Is this all remote and 'other worldly'? Or does it say something about how we live our daily lives here and now?

In chapter 6, Galatians applies this 'two ways' thinking to our method of daily living—our method of relating to each other. And it does this by looking at three specific applications: restoration, repayment, and reaping.

In each of these, it is contrasting two people—the legalist (the law keeper) and the Christian (the Spirit-led person).

a. Restoration

Investigate

Read Galatians 6:1-5

1. In what manner should you deal with a brother caught in sin?

2. What is the danger in doing this?

3. What should be your motivation in dealing with a brother caught in sin?

4. Does your brother's sin show your own spiritual superiority?

5. What should it show you?

Think it through

1. Does Paul contradict himself in verses 2 and 5? How can you fit these two ideas together?

2. How would you feel if you were "caught in a sin" (v.1) by a Christian brother or sister?

3. How would you want that brother or sister to treat you?

4. Picture this: you have discovered that a Christian friend of yours has fallen into the sin of adultery—what steps will you take to "gently restore them" (v.1)?

5. What excuses might they make for their behaviour?

6. How will you respond to those excuses?

7. What (if anything) will you say to other Christians?

8. How would a legalist (i.e. law-keeper) deal with someone who falls into sin?

b. Repayment

Investigate

Read Galatians 6:6

1. What does it mean to "share all good things" with your instructor (in the word of God)?

2. Is this optional? (v.6)

3. Does this necessarily apply only to money?

Think it through

1. List three ways in which you might be able to "share every good thing" with your teacher of God's word. (Be creative!)

1.

2.

3.

2. How might a legalist respond to the necessity of "sharing all things" with his or her instructor?

c. Reaping

Investigate

Read Galatians 6:7-10

1. Who controls this 'sowing and reaping' process? (v.7)

2. Some 'sow' (that is, invest their time, mind and energy) to please the sinful nature. What will they reap?

3. What will the one who 'sows' to please the Spirit reap?

4. Does the 'reaping' happen very soon after the 'sowing'?

5. Why do we reap what we sow?

6. When should we do good? (v.10)

7. To whom should we do good?

8. To whom should we give priority?

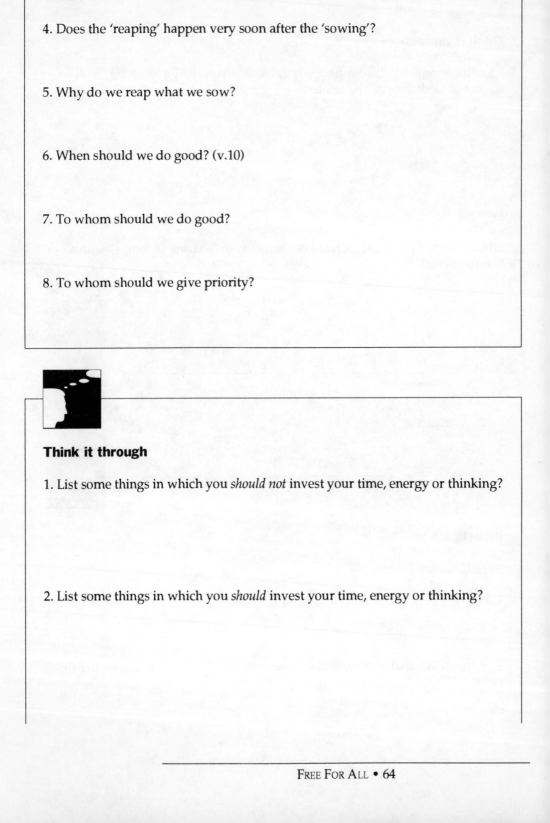

Think it through

1. List some things in which you *should not* invest your time, energy or thinking?

2. List some things in which you *should* invest your time, energy or thinking?

3. We all have limited financial resources, and much of the world is crying out in poverty and hunger for our help. Given the unlimited needs of the world, what priorities should you have in generously sharing your money? (Consult Gal 6:6, 6:10 and 1 Tim 5:8)

2. Parting words

As Paul closes his letter to the Galatians, he aims a few parting shots at those who are trying to compel the Galatians to submit to law. In doing so, he highlights the contrast there is between the gospel of grace and law-keeping, between the freedom of the Spirit and the slavery of legalism. His final words are worth thinking over as a fitting conclusion to all that Galatians has been saying.

Investigate

Read Galatians 6:11-18

1. Who are these legalists trying to impress?

2. What are these legalists trying to avoid?

3. What matters to Paul?

4. What doesn't matter to Paul?

5. How do these verses summarize the concerns of the whole letter?

6. Sum up what you have learned from your study of Galatians.

TELL US WHAT YOU THINK OF
Free For All

Free For All is the seventh in a series of Interactive Bible Studies. We'd like your comments and feedback so that we can continue to improve them as we go along. Please fill in the following questionnaire after you have completed the studies and return it to:

St Matthias Press, PO Box 225, KINGSFORD NSW 2032 or
St Matthias Press, PO Box 665, LONDON SW20 8RU

1. We don't want to know your name, but could you tell us your:
    sex _____ age _____ denomination _____

2. Are you a full-time Christian minister?
    ❏ yes ❏ no

3. Did you do the studies:
    ❏ by yourself
    ❏ with one or two others
    ❏ with a group of 5-10 others
    ❏ with a group of more than 10

4. Did you find the level of the studies:
    ❏ too low/simplistic
    ❏ about right
    ❏ too high-brow/intellectual

5. Did you feel that the studies were practical enough in their application?
    ❏ yes ❏ no

6. How long, on average, did each study take to work through (individually)?

    _____

7. If you did the study in a group, how long, on average, did you spend discussing each one?

    _____

8. Do you have any comments or suggestions about individual studies?
    Study no. | Comment

9. Do you have any overall comments or suggestions? (Write on the back if you need more room)

Galatians on Tape

For those who would like some further input on Galatians, a set of tapes is available which expounds the passages looked at in *Free For All*. These eight sermons by Phillip Jensen provide additional insights and ideas, and tie the material together in a way that is possible in a sermon, but not in a group Bible study.

The tapes are an ideal accompaniment to these studies, especially for group leaders who want to do some additional preparation.

Cost for the full set of eight tapes (including postage to anywhere in Australia) is $50. To place your order, phone us on (02) 663 1478 or write to the address below. Enclose a cheque with your order or, if you prefer, we can invoice you.

St Matthias Tapes
Reply Paid No. 4
PO Box 225
KINGSFORD   NSW   2032
(no stamp necessary if posted in Australia)

For those in England and Europe, please contact Tim Thornborough on (81) 947 5686 for details, or write to the address below.

St Matthias Press
PO Box 665
LONDON   SW20 8RU
ENGLAND

TOPICAL BIBLE STUDIES
New from St Matthias Press

Examining the teaching of the Scriptures on important topics

Cash Values (Money)

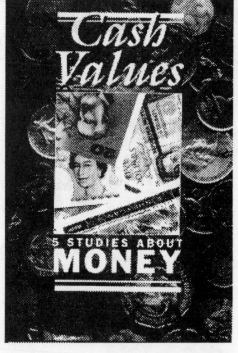

Money is a tricky topic for Christians, and we rarely sit down to carefully work out what the Bible has to tell us about it. *Cash Values* is designed to get us to do just that. In a series of short, thoroughly readable studies, Tony Payne guides us through the important Bible passages about money, all the time explaining how the subject is significant to our relationship with God and our fellowship with other Christians. Straightforward and punchy discussion blended with responsible attention to the Scriptures makes *Cash Values* a valuable resource for both churches and individuals. This is the first in a new series of Topical Bible Studies. Author: Tony Payne.

Also from St Matthias Press

Two Cities (Isaiah)

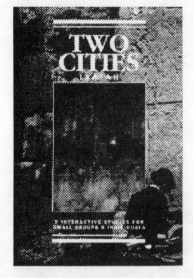

Too often we choose to ignore books like Isaiah, putting them in the 'too hard for Bible study' basket. And yet, Isaiah is frequently quoted in the New Testament and tells us much about God's plan of salvation. It's a book we should read.

Two Cities is designed to help us get a grip on—and to grip us with—the message of Isaiah. It cuts a highway through the 'branches', 'stumps' and 'deserts' that are scattered across Isaiah's terrain. It takes us to a two-way intersection and shows us the road to the city of destruction and the road to the city of God. Careful explanations of difficult passages and well-crafted, challenging questions make studying this crucial Old Testament book a whole lot less daunting. Authors: Andrew Reid and Karen Morris.

The One and Only (Deuteronomy)

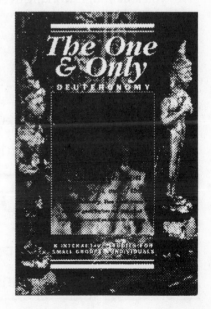

What do you say to a nation with a record of not listening? How can Moses persuade them to live a life worthy of the mercy God has shown them? Will they respond to Moses' charge to love God with all of their heart, soul and strength?

On one hand, Deuteronomy tells the story of a nation—their history, their laws, their way of life, their hopes and dreams. On the other hand, and most importantly, it is the story of their God, Yahweh, the creator of the universe, the One and Only.

The One and Only explores Deuteronomy with New Testament eyes. It leaves you with a picture of an awesome and wonderful God who has kept his promises and, in his Son, delivered salvation to his worldwide people, as we wait on the edge of a heavenly inheritance. Author: Bryson Smith.

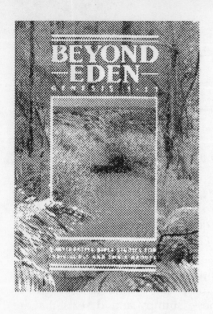

Beyond Eden

The first eleven chapters of the Bible are full of cataclysmic events — the creation of the world, the fall of mankind, the flood. But what is their significance for 20th (soon to be 21st) Century Christians? Looking back at Genesis from this side of the coming of Christ, what are we to make of it?

Beyond Eden leads you on a voyage of discovery to find life-changing answers to these questions.

Authors: Phillip Jensen & Tony Payne.

The Path to Godliness

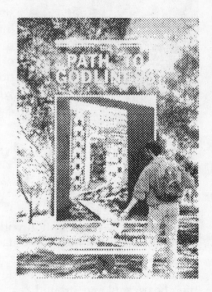

If the idea of being godly is attractive, how can we turn our vague yearning for it into reality?

In Paul's short letter to Titus, God reveals the path to true godliness. We are warned about false trails and given stirring encouragement about the source of true godliness, its motivation and the shape it will take. Titus is not a long letter, but it gives you a thorough working over.

Authors: Phillip Jensen & Tony Payne.

Other titles available: *The Complete Christian* (Colossians), *The Path to Godliness* (Titus). More titles coming soon—ring for details.